Queen of Sheba

A Captivating Guide to a Mysterious Queen Mentioned in the Bible and Her Relationship with King Solomon

© Copyright 2019

All Rights Reserved. No part of this book may be reproduced in any form without permission in writing from the author. Reviewers may quote brief passages in reviews.

Disclaimer: No part of this publication may be reproduced or transmitted in any form or by any means, mechanical or electronic, including photocopying or recording, or by any information storage and retrieval system, or transmitted by email without permission in writing from the publisher.

While all attempts have been made to verify the information provided in this publication, neither the author nor the publisher assumes any responsibility for errors, omissions or contrary interpretations of the subject matter herein.

This book is for entertainment purposes only. The views expressed are those of the author alone and should not be taken as expert instruction or commands. The reader is responsible for his or her own actions.

Adherence to all applicable laws and regulations, including international, federal, state and local laws governing professional licensing, business practices, advertising and all other aspects of doing business in the US, Canada, UK or any other jurisdiction is the sole responsibility of the purchaser or reader.

Neither the author nor the publisher assumes any responsibility or liability whatsoever on the behalf of the purchaser or reader of these materials. Any perceived slight of any individual or organization is purely unintentional.

Free Bonus from Captivating History (Available for a Limited time)

Hi History Lovers!

Now you have a chance to join our exclusive history list so you can get your first history ebook for free as well as discounts and a potential to get more history books for free! Simply visit the link below to join.

Captivatinghistory.com/ebook

Also, make sure to follow us on Facebook, Twitter and Youtube by searching for Captivating History.

The queen of the south shall rise up in the judgment with the men of this generation, and condemn them: for she came from the utmost parts of the earth to hear the wisdom of Solomon; and, behold, a greater than Solomon is here.

- Luke 11:31

Contents

INTRODUCTION 1
CHAPTER 1 – SHEBA BEFORE THE QUEEN 3
CHAPTER 2 – THE SHADOW OF THE SERPENT KING 7
CHAPTER 3 – A QUESTIONING QUEEN 11
CHAPTER 4 – WORD OF THE WISE KING 15
CHAPTER 5 – A JOURNEY TO ISRAEL 19
CHAPTER 6 – ENCOUNTERING SOLOMON 24
CHAPTER 7 – A FORBIDDEN UNION 28
CHAPTER 8 – JOY ON THE JOURNEY HOME 33
CHAPTER 9 – A NEW KING 38
CONCLUSION 43
SOURCES 47

Introduction

Writing a biography for the Queen of Sheba is quickly complicated by a simple roadblock: the fact that historians aren't sure that this mysterious queen ever even existed.

To start with, the events detailed in the story of the queen took place so long ago that written records of that time and place barely exist except in the form of religious manuscripts. The Queen of Sheba reigned around 950 BCE, nearly 3,000 years ago, and written records from the areas where Sheba could have existed are few and far between. The records we do have telling the story of the queen come from three major religions: Islam, Christianity, and Judaism. In the holy texts from these religions—including the *Kebra Nagast* from Ethiopia, the Hebrew Bible's Books of Chronicles, the Holy Bible, the Quran, and the Jewish Antiquities—accounts of the Queen of Sheba center on one major event in her life: her visit with King Solomon of Israel. Even here, the accounts differ wildly on what exactly the nature of her encounter with the wise king was.

The most detailed record of the queen's life lies in the *Kebra Nagast*. This Ethiopian text, whose title translates to "The Glory of Kings," is also of unknown origin; however, it was intensely important to Ethiopian emperors of the Solomonic dynasty and became an integral part of Orthodox Christianity in Ethiopia. In this book, the Queen of Sheba's visit to King Solomon morphs from a quest for wisdom into a romantic encounter, and it eventually results in a union that would produce a dynasty that lasted for millennia. Ancient Ethiopian mythology also mentions a courageous warrior maiden, a virgin who faced down despicable monsters and who bore the same name—and existed in the same timeframe—as the Queen of Sheba mentioned in the holy texts.

Archaeological evidence, however, barely points to an existence of Sheba at all, let alone providing any evidence of a queen somewhere along its timeline.

Piecing together an account of the queen's life from these varied sources gives one a fascinating glimpse into the ancient world, and from the turmoil of this chaos of information rises one constant figure: the queen herself. In every account, she is bold and wise, fearless and selfless. She strives to bring peace and protection to her country. She faces monsters on behalf of the innocent masses, and she finds herself in power even though female rulers were rare in her era. And instead of backing away from the responsibility, she seizes it with two hands. She travels the world seeking wisdom, and when she finds love instead, she has the courage to unselfishly turn her back on that love and journey back to a home that she has promised to care for. At every turn, the Queen of Sheba remains one of the earliest symbols of female power, and her story—her legend—still serves to be a fascinating and inspiring one, one that speaks to hearts and minds even today, whether it is myth or history.

Chapter 1 – Sheba Before the Queen

The first thing that we don't really know about the Queen of Sheba is where exactly Sheba was. Historians have been puzzling for generations over the location of this mysterious land; considering that the queen herself visited Solomon in around 950 BCE, it's no easy question to answer. Guesses have included Yemen, southern Arabia, and parts of Africa. However, the legends and traditions that include the most detail and that align most closely with the biblical account of the Queen of Sheba point to Sheba being one of the oldest kingdoms in the entire world: Ethiopia.

An Ancient Nation

Ethiopia is the oldest independent country on the African continent. Its rich history goes back for thousands of years, with one of its most prominent beginnings being the Kingdom of Aksum in 100 CE. But Ethiopia's story begins much, much earlier than that. According to the story of the Queen of Sheba, this unique and ancient country was already a vast and wealthy nation a thousand years before the name of Aksum would ever be spoken. This is unsurprising considering that Ethiopia may be one of the first places in the world to be inhabited by human beings. It is speculated that the Garden of Eden itself may have been located somewhere in Ethiopia, and science has proven that some of the earliest human tribes lived in this beautiful and ancient country.

The furthest reaches of the history of Ethiopia have long since been lost to the 3,000 years between the Queen of Sheba's reign and the modern day. The earliest mentions of this kingdom come from the same book that describes the Queen of Sheba's visit to Solomon: The Holy Bible.

The Origins of Ethiopia According to the Bible

The Book of Genesis details the creation of the world and of mankind itself. It also tells the story of how the first two children born in the newly minted universe—Cain and Abel, the two sons of Adam—divided the human race in half when it was still in its very infancy. Cast out of the Garden of Eden because of the sins of Adam and his wife Eve, the world's first family found themselves tilling the earth to survive. A bout of jealousy rose up between the two brothers, and in a fit of terrible rage, Cain killed his own brother. The world's first murder had been committed.

According to the Bible and to an ancient Ethiopian Christian text, the *Kebra Nagast*, which contains the most detailed account of the life of the Queen of Sheba, the descendants of Cain and Seth, their younger brother who followed in Abel's footsteps, remained divided. While the descendants of Seth became leaders, the descendants of Cain developed into barbaric nations, eventually becoming so unutterably abominable in the sight of God that they were washed away in the Great Flood. Only a descendant of Seth—Noah—and his family survived.

It is here, right after the description of the Great Flood, where we find the origin of Ethiopia itself according to these two ancient texts. According to the King James Bible:

> Now these are the generations of the sons of Noah, Shem, Ham, and Japheth: and unto them were sons born after the flood. [...] By these were the isles of the Gentiles divided in their lands; everyone after his tongue, after their families, in their nations. And the sons of Ham; **Cush**, and Mizraim, and Phut, and Canaan. And the sons of **Cush**; Seba, and Havilah, and Sabtah, and Raamah, and Sabtechah: and the sons of Raamah; **Sheba**, and Dedan.
>
> – Genesis 10:1 and 5-9

"Cush" is an ancient name for Ethiopia, and as this passage notes that nations grew from these prominent families, it is easy to imagine that Ethiopia may have developed from the descendants of Cush. In fact, a group of languages still spoken in Ethiopia today is still referred to as the "Cushitic languages." Somewhere along the line, Cush's descendant Sheba may have loaned his name to the nation that would be formed by his offspring, and so the Sheba whose queen became so famous might have been born.

Sheba and D'mt

The very first mention of Ethiopia is found in the hieroglyphs of the ancient Egyptians, dating back to about 2500 BCE. There it is spoken of as the land of Punt, a country where Egyptian merchants were able to find an abundance of trade, particularly in gold. The exact location of Punt has not been ascertained, but it was likely somewhere in the northern regions of modern-day Ethiopia.

Fast forward several hundred years into the Iron Age, and one finds the first confirmed kingdom that was established in the area of Ethiopia. Details about this kingdom are sketchy and shadowy, wreathed in the mists of distant history, but its name survives: D'mt. It was likely formed somewhere between 1000 and 700 BCE, and even the nature of its inhabitants remains a mystery to this day. While many of them were likely indigenous people from the area, there was also probably a high proportion of Sabaean people. The

Sabaeans were a south Arabic people from an area of modern-day Yemen, another region which has also been proposed as being the Sheba of the Bible, although its accounts of the Queen of Sheba are not as richly detailed as that of the Ethiopians.

D'mt itself may have been the kingdom ruled over by the Queen of Sheba herself or was possibly even a neighboring kingdom; Sheba and D'mt, at any rate, existed at the same time, although they may not have been the same kingdom. The people of D'mt left only a few inscriptions behind, and even fewer archaeological expeditions have been conducted in order to find out more about this ancient kingdom. Their legacy lives on mostly in the ruins of mighty temples built from impressive stone.

Sheba at the Time of the Queen

Only one thing can be known for certain about the Kingdom of Sheba at the time when its famous queen was born: it had to have been rich—inexpressibly rich. Considering that it was conveniently located on a trade route that would have put it in touch with powers such as ancient Egypt and the might of Israel, this is no great surprise. Ethiopia was also a land rich in all kinds of natural resources with great stretches of fertile land and gold running rich in its rivers and earth. It was into this rich and flourishing land—somewhere in the 10th century BCE—that the legendary queen would be born. Yet abundant though her surroundings must have been, the queen's ascension to the throne could not have been easy. For she became queen the same way that all monarchs ascended in those days: by a death in the family.

Chapter 2 – The Shadow of the Serpent King

Awre towered above the city of Aksum, the scaly length of his terrifying body rising above the buildings, screams echoing from wall to wall as his slender shadow fell across the length and breadth of the entire city. His jaws gaped open, great fangs curving from them, a crown glittering on his flat head above two brilliant eyes that were frighteningly human in the face of a monstrous snake. A forked tongue stabbed at the sky, moving as swift and sinuous as the curves of the monster as Awre slithered through the streets, his foul breath preceding him like a portent of the deaths that were to come.

The people of Aksum didn't think. They just grabbed their children and fled. They all knew that dreaded silhouette on the horizon far too well—Awre had been terrorizing the city for years, devouring livestock by the hundreds. Cattle and sheep, camels and chickens—they were all the same to Awre's insatiable appetite. But on this day, the people fled with a special fear in their hearts. A fear that was for more than just their livestock.

Awre's lashing tail smashed into the corner of a building. Crumbling stone rained down on the street, and a young mother screamed, snatching up her little daughter out of the path of the falling debris. She stared up at the shape of the monster as it went past and cowered into the niche of the doorway, clutching her little girl as tightly as she could. She knew what day it was. She knew that someone's daughter was about to be taken. Because despite the vast number of animals that Awre consumed, their flesh was not enough for the serpent king. Once a year, he demanded something more, a special treat to allay his bloodthirst: the sacrifice of a human being—and not just any human being, but a pure and beautiful virgin girl.

Now, he continued down the streets, his deep laugh rocking the foundations of the houses as he slithered eagerly toward his annual feast. He saw her silhouette waiting for him on a designated hilltop. Her curves were as slender as his were scaly, but even from this distance, he could see that there was something different about her. The girls normally screamed and wept. This one stood on the top of the hill with her feet planted wide apart and her arms folded, and as he drew closer, he saw something burning brightly in her eyes. It wasn't fear. It was fire.

The girl's skin blazed like ebony in the midday sun, her brown eyes were alight, and her shining black hair was swept back and pinned down by the weight of her bejeweled tiara. Surprised, the serpent king came to a halt, rising up so that he stood over his quarry. She met his eyes with a defiance that he had never seen before.

"Makeda, the Princess of Sheba?" Awre was as surprised as he was amused. "If your people think that sacrificing a young woman so beautiful and of such high rank will sate my appetite for longer than the usual year, they are sadly mistaken." He lowered his head, his forked tongue flicking out only inches from her beautiful face. "Yet I will not deny that you will make a wonderful meal."

Makeda raised her chin. There was nothing but cool determination in her face. "I will make your last one," she murmured.

Awre laughed. Then he reared back his head, opened his jaws wide, and struck. So did Makeda. With the swiftness of the serpent that she hoped to conquer, she grasped the ugly horn that curled from the tip of his snout. Her hand reached into the front of her dress and pulled out a dagger that cut the sunshine with its sharpness. The dagger flashed, and blood burst down the front of Awre's throat. The serpent king reared back, ripping his horn from Makeda's hands, and he tried to take a deep breath to roar, but his throat was cut. He could not even scream in pain. He just fell backward and collapsed, the whole terrible length of him falling at Makeda's feet. Sheba was saved from his scourge forever.

* * * *

The birthday of the Queen of Sheba has been lost, as has most of the details about her childhood. All we really have is this legend about a girl named Makeda, a name meaning *not thus*; perhaps because she would later become known for converting her people from their indigenous faith (which, according to the Quran, was the worship of the sun) to monotheism, likely Judaism. She probably earned the name by telling the people that "not thus is it good (to worship the sun or stars)," pointing them in the direction of monotheism instead.

All this, however, was far in the future. Princess Makeda probably did not single-handedly slay a monstrous monarch, but the fable must have arisen from a young woman of exceptional fortitude and resourcefulness. As a princess, Makeda had already proven herself to be an intelligent and determined young woman who knew what she wanted and would stop at nothing to get it, especially when it came to protecting her people.

Her early life in the royal capital of Sheba (which might have been modern-day Yeha, as evidenced by numerous ruins built by the people of D'mt) was a privileged one. Sheba was a ridiculously wealthy kingdom made rich by an abundance of gold, spices, and other priceless treasures carried off by its merchants to other great powers of the ancient world. Makeda had everything she could have possibly wanted, and with her father on the throne, her future was stable.

Or so she thought. In the ancient world, kingdoms were often ruled over by kings and not by queens. Compared to their male counterparts, queens had very little power. Wars were fought and alliances made by the kings of all the countries who had absolute power over all of their subjects, including their royal wives. Having a queen on the throne without a king was unthinkable, but it was about to happen and in a manner that would bring tragedy to Makeda's young life.

It is likely that Makeda was still a young woman when the current king of Sheba either died or was somehow removed from the throne, probably in an unexpected manner. The end of his reign threatened to cast the entire kingdom of Sheba into chaos. With no one to lead them, what would become of the people? Their riches were a liability now, with power-hungry rulers on every side ready to invade and plunder the coffers that Makeda's father had worked so hard to protect. If a strong ruler failed to take the throne, Sheba and its people would be doomed.

So, Makeda did what she was fabled to have done on the hilltops of Aksum. She saw that her people were in trouble. And she stepped up to protect them. She was crowned the Queen of Sheba and suddenly became possibly the most powerful woman in all of her known world.

Chapter 3 – A Questioning Queen

Illustration I: The Queen of Sheba as depicted in a 15th-century illuminated manuscript

Now on the throne of the mighty nation of Sheba, Makeda had restored stability and security to her country simply by her ascension. It appears that Sheba continued to prosper during her reign; trade was bustling, and the country's mines continued to overflow with abundant gold.

Yet the young queen was not wholly content upon her throne. She had never been raised to rule a kingdom—she lacked the lifelong education that a young man in her position would have received in being groomed for kingship as the crown prince. Now, although she maintained admirable control over Sheba, Makeda longed desperately for a mentor. She had no one to ask when she was uncertain about something, no experience to fall back on when difficult decisions came her way, and as the ruling queen, difficult decisions were a daily part of her job description.

There was something else that Makeda yearned for, too, although this was a more subconscious longing. Her mind and sense of duty wanted a mentor, someone to guide her through all of the twists and turns that her queenly path was taking. But her heart had needs and desires of its own.

Little did she know that, 2,000 miles away, her heart's desire was waiting on the throne of Jerusalem.

* * * *

King Solomon had big shoes to fill.

His father was David—a name that had become legendary long before David ever became king. A shepherd boy who had become a killer of giants, a renowned warrior, a mighty king, and "a man after God's own heart," King David was the golden boy of the golden age of Israel. He led the nation out of the darkness of King Saul's reign, despite Saul's multiple attempts to murder him, and David's long reign had been illustrious.

Solomon was not King David's firstborn son. Instead, he was the result of King David's greatest mistake: committing adultery with a beautiful woman named Bathsheba and having her husband killed in battle so that he could marry her. Solomon should have been a pariah, an outcast, a scapegoat for the sins of his father. Instead, according to Nathan the Prophet, Solomon was God's favorite among David's children. David accepted Nathan's prophecy and groomed Solomon to become the heir to his throne, and when age and infirmity confined David to his bedchamber, Solomon was crowned King of Israel.

It had been years now since Solomon had taken the throne. The early days of his rule had not been easy with conspirators rising up against him and even his own older brother trying to seize power, but Solomon had succeeded in establishing himself as the king. And he was proving himself to be a king unlike any other. According to the Bible, God had appeared to Solomon in a dream, asking him what he wanted: "Ask what I shall give thee."

Solomon could have asked for anything. Power, wealth, glory—but instead, the young king wanted only one thing: wisdom. "Give therefore thy servant an understanding heart to judge thy people, that I may discern between good and bad: for who is able to judge this thy so great a people?" he asked. His prayer was answered, and Solomon's wisdom became renowned throughout the ancient world.

Now, Solomon was reigning comfortably over his vast nation. While he had failed to ask God for wealth when he'd given his request for wisdom, he had become almost immeasurably rich. Thousands of chariot horses pranced in his stables; Egypt and Philistia, the historical enemies of Israel, now paid him tribute. Times of peace and plenty had come, and Solomon was able to turn his mind to a mission that had been given to him even before he was born.

David had always wanted to build a great temple to the God of Israel, but God had forbidden him from doing so because David was a man of war, instead telling David that he would give the task to his son since he would be a peaceful ruler. While Solomon was a great king, the same as his father was, this was where much of the similarities between the two men ended. History knows them best by their writings, which is a great example of the differences between them. David wrote the Psalms, an emotive, passionate, often desperate collection of songs whose lyrics are often raw. Solomon, on the other hand, wrote the Proverbs, which soberly sets out wise instructions for his son. Wild and warlike David may have forged a kingdom, but he was not fit to build the first and most wonderful temple in Jerusalem.

Solomon, on the other hand, was as intelligent and grounded as he was wise, and he knew that building this temple would be his duty. So, he started to gather the materials for the temple, and this was a task that could have only been performed by this wealthiest of kings. He would need wood, gold, priceless fabrics, precious stones, and shining metals in almost unimaginable proportions. And he would need to search the farthest reaches of the known world in order to find everything he needed. He would search throughout Israel, even into Egypt and Assyria, and perhaps even across the Mediterranean.

Perhaps even as far as Sheba.

Chapter 4 – Word of the Wise King

Tamrin had been all over the known world. He had walked the Silk Road to the borders of China, bringing back priceless Asian treasures to his beloved queen; wandered the barren deserts of Arabia; beheld the majesty of the pyramids and the riches of the pharaohs; and lived in the magnificence that was Sheba at the time of Queen Makeda. Yet the one place that he hadn't yet seen was Israel. Tamrin was an educated merchant, and he'd heard much about the place. It was a strange country, he had learned, a place where all of its citizens worshiped only one god, and where there were no astrologers, no magicians, and no soothsayers allowed. As his dhows, some of the swiftest cargo ships in the world, parted the waters of the Red Sea, Tamrin gazed to the east, eagerly anticipating his first sighting of this new land.

Israel had never been on his usual trade route before. In fact, it was a promising—and mysterious—request that brought him in this direction. Solomon, the peculiar but extremely wealthy king of Israel, had sent out a request to merchants all over the world asking for their most precious and expensive materials in huge quantities. He had gold and silver aplenty, he said; he wanted building materials, and only the very best would do. Alloys of gold mixed with copper so that it gleamed red. Sapphires. Ebony. Tamrin had seen splendid buildings in Sheba, and he had handled almost incomprehensibly valuable cargoes before, but the reason behind this king's request was puzzling. Solomon wanted to build a temple—a gigantic, magnificent temple, even bigger and more beautiful than his own royal palace.

Tamrin didn't understand, but he did recognize a business opportunity when he saw one. And so, when King Solomon's request had reached him, he didn't hesitate to set sail for Israel with his dhows wallowing low in the water, laden heavily with every treasure he could find within the borders of Sheba and along the rest of his trade route. His was one of the largest fleets of all of Sheba with more than seventy ships surrounding his own, all of them bearing expensive cargo. He could only hope that this Israelite king was as rich as he seemed to think he was.

When Tamrin arrived in Jerusalem, the capital of Israel and the seat of its king, he realized that the accounts of Solomon's wealth and wisdom had not been exaggerated. The port where he left his dhows had been utterly teeming with merchant vessels; his short journey inland to Jerusalem itself had taken him through fields of growing crops with fattened cattle grazing on all of the hills. Approaching Jerusalem had been as awe-inspiring as it was intimidating. The city towered above the rest of the landscape, resting on a rocky hill. Its walls and buttresses were imposing, the gleaming armor of its soldiers a threat to any who dared to oppose it. These soldiers were battle-hardened veterans, too; Tamrin had seen many with scars, relics from the terrible wars that King David had fought against the Philistines and other enemies. More recently, a civil war had gripped the country when David's own son Absalom had risen up against him.

But Absalom was long gone now. The Philistines had been reduced to tributaries, and Solomon had taken Absalom's place as heir to the throne. The soldiers stood motionless and idle, their weapons sheathed, and the city gates had been thrown wide open to the stream of merchants making their laborious way up the hills. Mules and donkeys, camels and oxen, filled the road, all of them bearing heavy loads of wonderful materials in such abundance that Tamrin could only stare. His hundreds of camels were not the only beasts of burden to carry expensive goods up this hill. Leading his caravan, Tamrin sneaked glances at the other merchants around him. The animals were carrying ingots of bronze, great rolls of purple fabric, and planks of Lebanon cedar. Whatever reasons this king had for building a temple, he was going to build a truly magnificent one.

When Tamrin reached Solomon's palace, he already felt like his eyeballs might fall out of his head from staring. The streets of Jerusalem were filled with people, and they all seemed to be so happy; there was music on every street corner, laughing vendors doing brisk business with chattering women, and children chasing one another through the streets. The palace itself was an awesome sight, its towering pillars richly decorated with all kinds of precious metals and brilliant fabrics.

Once Tamrin's camels and their burdens had been taken care of, he made his way into the palace where he was received by Solomon himself. The king had decided to personally oversee all of the operations regarding the building of the temple, and that included speaking to the merchants that had brought materials from far-off lands. Tamrin realized that he was nervous about meeting this famous king, which surprised him; as a personal friend of Queen Makeda, he was no stranger to royalty. But there was something a little terrifying about the wealth and power that was evident in Solomon's court. He wiped his sweating hands on his robes before daring to approach the throne room.

The room itself was dazzling beyond compare. The steps leading up to the throne were decorated with golden lions, and the floor gleamed in shining marble. The king who sat upon the throne was broad-shouldered, his beard tumbling to his chest, the line of his jaw as stern and formidable as the walls surrounding his palace. Yet, when Tamrin bowed low, the voice that told him to rise held a gentleness that he hadn't been expecting. He looked into the king's eyes for the first time and was surprised to see humility there. Solomon's speech was gentle, and when he sent a servant girl to bring wine and bread to the tired merchant, his request was spoken softly. A little speechless, Tamrin automatically went through the motions of discussing the merchandise that he had brought to Solomon and negotiating a price, but his mind was occupied with other things.

Firstly, he had been all over the world but never stepped foot in a kingdom quite like Solomon's Israel. And secondly, Queen Makeda had told him how much she had wanted to find a mentor that could guide her through the monumental task of governing a kingdom like Sheba. Tamrin was pretty sure he'd just stumbled upon the perfect person for that task.

Chapter 5 – A Journey to Israel

Tamrin had been back for a few days already, and all he ever spoke of was the wisdom of King Solomon.

Queen Makeda, who was a friend of the merchant, received him every morning to hear more about his travels all the way to Jerusalem and back. At first, she was slightly amused by the enthusiasm with which Tamrin spoke of the grand country he had visited, its incredible architecture, its happy people, and most of all, its wise king. Tamrin was usually not one to gush, as he was a weathered, seasoned, battle-scarred man who had seen it all and survived everything. Yet there was a light in his eyes that Makeda had never seen before, and after a few days of listening to his stories, it began to fascinate her. She found herself asking about everything he'd seen, and there was one part of all his stories that interested her more than anything else: Solomon.

Makeda knew that Tamrin had done business with most of the great powers of her ancient world. Yet he had never seemed so awestruck before as he was now. What struck Makeda the most was that Tamrin was impressed with King Solomon not for his wealth or his good looks or his military prowess—in fact, Tamrin said, King Solomon had never once been to war. Instead, the merchant was awed by the king's wisdom. In an age when world leaders came to power based solely on their parentage, foolish kings were in abundance. Many of the monarchs in power at the time were selfish, power-hungry, and occasionally even insane. But not Solomon, Tamrin told Makeda. He was more than just a good king—he held a wisdom, a depth of knowledge and intelligence that Tamrin had never seen before. As much as Solomon's coffers overflowed with gold, Tamrin told the queen, his mind overflowed with wisdom. His judgments were always just, yet there was a humility in him, a willingness to learn from others and a gentleness in his dealings with his servants, that was rare to see in people of any rank.

The more that Tamrin talked about Solomon, the more Makeda became enamored with this king that she had never met. While all was going well in her kingdom, she was still feeling lost and alone in her haughty position. There was no one to guide her, no princely education to draw upon; Makeda felt like she was winging it, flying blind with the fate of her people at stake. Solomon seemed to be the opposite of her. He had grown up in the shadow of the mightiest king that Israel had ever had, and he seemed to be so sure of this God that his people served. If what he said was true, this God of his had given him wisdom that surpassed anything even the well-traveled Tamrin had seen before. Makeda wasn't so sure of this God of Israel, but she was sure of one thing: Tamrin was different after spending time with Solomon, and she wanted whatever it was that Solomon had that made him capable of ruling with such calm confidence.

Every day, Makeda summoned Tamrin up to her palace and listened to everything that he had to say, her eyes wide and rapt as she hung on his every word. Sometimes she cried when Tamrin told her of the things that Solomon had done and said. Tamrin assumed that she was just awed and took pleasure in the things that he said, but perhaps there was something else that caused the queen to weep, something more inconsolable: a desperate yearning to be able to do what Solomon could do. Makeda wanted to rule better, and she wanted to know the answers to the deep questions in her heart, questions that she could no longer ask of her parents because they were gone.

At last, after listening to hundreds of Tamrin's stories about his time in Jerusalem, Makeda made up her mind. Everything was peaceful and stable in Sheba, but it might not always remain that way. She needed to learn more about how to be a good monarch and how to care for her people well. There were no two ways about it: The Queen of Sheba had to meet King Solomon. No matter how arduous the journey might be, Makeda was determined to make it, for the good of her kingdom.

* * * *

Queen Makeda faced the crowds of her people, her heart fluttering with nervousness. She knew by the adoration in their eyes that they placed their trust in her, yet part of her was terrified by their trust, feeling in her heart that she was unworthy of it. But they couldn't know that. They had to believe in a strong and courageous queen, so she kept her back straight and her chin up as she addressed them.

"Hearken, O ye who are my people," she began, "and give ye ear to my words. For I desire wisdom…"

The people listened attentively, every eye and ear fixed upon their queen as she spoke. She had worked hard on her speech, and she gave it with confidence, telling them about the riches and goodness of the wisdom that she sought after so earnestly. She spoke of its sweetness, its strength, and its value, calling it "the best of all treasures." "I will follow in the footprints of wisdom, and she shall protect me forever," Queen Makeda told her people. "I will seek after wisdom, and she shall be with me forever."

Her voice grew softer as she went on, and a wistful quality crept into them as she began to extol the virtues of a wise person. "By the sight of him thou shalt become wise," she said. "Hearken to the utterance of his mouth, so that thou mayest become like unto him." She lowered her eyes, longing creeping into her tone. "And I love him merely on hearing concerning him," she almost whispered, "and without seeing him, and the whole story of him that hath been told to me is to me as the desire of my heart, and like water to the thirsty man."

Silence fell, and Makeda's heart flipped over. The last sentence she'd spoken had been almost to herself; it was not a part of the speech that she had so carefully planned. She froze, holding her breath as her people gazed at her. Had they seen the emotion that had suddenly overtaken her? Did they think her weak?

But her people's reaction was favorable. They admired her commitment to seeking out more knowledge, and they pledged their loyalty to her and their dedication to whichever cause she saw fit to invest her time in. Makeda, hugely relieved, at once started to make preparations to leave. This was no small task. As the queen of a powerful and wealthy country like Sheba, Makeda knew that she had to arrive in Jerusalem with a suitable amount of majesty and ceremony. She was the ultimate ambassador for Sheba, and it was her duty to show off its strength as well as she could so that Israel would see it as a useful ally instead of an easy enemy to overthrow. She could not afford to anger Israel, but neither could she allow Sheba to look weak in comparison. As much as she had loved hearing all of Tamrin's stories about Solomon, she was by no means a fool. Her heart might be falling for him, but her mind was still suspicious that perhaps Tamrin had been exaggerating after all. She would have to test this king carefully before she could learn from him, and she would have to be diplomatic in her dealings with him.

To achieve her goal of impressing Israel while maintaining friendly relations with the mighty nation, Makeda had a massive gift prepared for Solomon from the riches of her country: gold, precious stones, and an enormous amount of spices. It took almost 800 camels, alongside plenty of mules and donkeys, to load up all of the precious items that the queen was taking to Israel. And so, in a great train of beasts of burden—as unlike Tamrin, the queen would be traveling on land—Makeda and her vast number of attendants set forth.

She did look back once, gazing at the green jewel that was Sheba, as she prepared to head into the desert that lay between her country and Israel. For a moment, all she wanted was to run back to her safe palace and hope that her knowledge would be enough to face whatever challenges her reign had yet to bring. But something was calling her north; her heart was dragging her in the direction of this wise king who could answer all of her questions. So, she looked ahead again and kept her eyes fixed forward until the dust cloud of their passing swallowed them whole.

Chapter 6 – Encountering Solomon

Illustration II: Solomon and the Queen of Sheba by Giovanni de Min. The queen's appearance is unlikely to be ethnically correct in this illustration.

Things could hardly have gotten any better for King Solomon, yet somehow, he felt that there was something missing.

The great project to which the king had devoted years of planning and construction, the Holy Temple he'd built in Jerusalem to the God of Israel, was complete at last. Hundreds of men had worked together to produce it, and precious materials had been gathered from all around the known world in order to build it. Solomon sat on his throne, remembering the terrifying and magnificent day that the Spirit of God had appeared to him in the Holy Temple, announcing His presence there. He knew that he'd completed what his father David had started and that his reign was already one of the most awe-inspiring in the ancient world. There were no enemies standing against Israel; King Hiram of Tyre had helped him to build the temple, and even the Pharaoh of Egypt, the ruler whose ancestors had once held the Israelites captive, had conquered the Canaanites on King Solomon's behalf and even given his own daughter in marriage to Solomon. The king himself was living in the lap of luxury. His people were prospering, and so was he, with stables full of priceless horses, treasuries piled with mountains of gold and silver, and houses filled with wives and concubines. He had everything he could possibly have wanted—except he didn't. There was something that he hadn't yet found in his wives or his wealth or his wisdom, and he didn't know yet what it was.

He thought back to the merchant that had brought some of the materials he'd used to build the temple: Tamrin, a dark-skinned, quick-witted man who had the look of a seasoned traveler and adventurer about him. He was suspicious of everyone, except there was one person that he seemed to hold in the highest regard: his queen, Makeda. Solomon wondered what made her so different that Tamrin would respect her so much. Was she perhaps a tyrant who inspired fear in her subjects? It seemed like the wonderful things that Tamrin had told him about her were far too good to be true.

Solomon didn't know. But he hoped, one day, to find out.

* * * *

When that day came, Solomon was awed.

King Solomon's throne room was beautifully decorated, as was befitting for the magnificence of the rest of his city. Its floor gleamed, constructed out of glass so finely polished that it shimmered like water. Details about the rest of the room have been lost to history, but there were likely pillars of expensive wood carved in fine detail, as well as purple draping and a gilded throne.

He watched from the windows of the splendid room as the great train of camels made its way toward his city on the hill. There were hundreds of them—he had never seen so many camels together before, not even with all his pomp and majesty. Tied one to another with goat hair ropes, the camels plodded contentedly along despite the tremendous burdens that they carried on their colorful saddles. Some of them had baby camels strapped onto their backs; Solomon knew that the mother camels were right behind those carrying the babies, and it made him think that they must have had a long journey. He sent his servants to find out who was bringing this great train of camels to his city, and when they returned, his heart flipped. It was the Queen of Sheba—the same queen who had made even Tamrin's cynical eyes light up when he spoke of her.

Solomon waited impatiently in his throne room as the train arrived. At last, he could hear the footsteps in the passage outside, and he gripped the arms of his throne in anticipation. The queen he had heard so much about was finally here.

The great doors swung open, and with attendants all around her, there she was, tall and stunning, her dark skin fascinating as it was an unusual sight for Solomon. Makeda's eyes were nervous, but her bearing was as fearless as it was proud. Her beautifully embroidered garment flowed down her slender curves, and Solomon felt awestruck as he looked at her in a way that had nothing to do with her rank and riches.

Solomon had just enough presence of mind to invite Makeda to approach the throne. She stepped forward then hesitated, spotting her reflection in the smooth glass floor. It seemed to give her pause for a moment. She gripped the front of her heavy skirt and lifted it, revealing slender ankles, and then stepped cautiously forward, toe first. She seemed startled when her foot met the cold, hard surface of the glass. Looking up at Solomon, there was a moment of awkwardness in her bearing.

The king realized that she'd first thought the glass floor was water. He hurried to reassure her, inviting her in, and she regained her composure and approached. When she reached the throne, she bowed low, her attendants all following suit. The Queen of Sheba had met King Solomon at last, and she was more than ready to test him with all of her questions. The first of which probably being what on Earth had possessed him to construct his floor out of the smoothest glass she had ever seen.

* * * *

The accounts regarding the Queen of Sheba's entrance into Jerusalem differ strongly. While both Jewish and Muslim works tell the story of the glass floor, Ethiopian manuscripts don't mention the floor at all. The Muslim account tells of demons warning Solomon that the Queen of Sheba had jinn blood in her, causing Solomon to construct the glass floor specially to trick Makeda into lifting her skirt and showing him unnaturally hairy, inhuman legs. The Bible itself does not go into detail about their first meeting, only mentioning her entrance into Jerusalem with a large gift of spices and precious metals for Solomon.

All the accounts, however, agree on one thing: Makeda's reason for visiting the venerated king. She was there to test his wisdom with her questions and decide whether she could learn from him the way Tamrin had promised. And young though she was, the queen was ready to test Solomon to his limits.

Chapter 7 – A Forbidden Union

Makeda had been in Jerusalem for several days, still resting from her journey, and even she was amazed at the sumptuousness of the quarters that Solomon had given her.

She and all her attendants had been given rooms within the royal palace itself: spacious places, beautifully decorated and elegantly furnished. That was not the end of Solomon's hospitality, however. Every day, he sent them more food than they could have ever possibly needed. Bread and oxen, fine white meal cooked in delicious gravy, wine and honey, fat poultry and mutton—even the delicacies that the king himself indulged in were sent to Makeda's quarters, accompanied by singers and entertainers. Makeda had grown up in the lap of luxury and never wanted for anything material, but this was more than even she was used to, and she found herself enjoying her rest.

Yet she hadn't come to Jerusalem to be fed and entertained. She had come to see the king. Not much time passed before Makeda asked for an audience with him, which was quickly granted.

Once again, Makeda went to meet King Solomon in the throne room. This time, however, as she walked inside, there was none of the awkwardness and nerves that she'd shown the first time. She stepped out boldly on the glass floor, and Solomon knew what was coming next: Makeda was going to test him with riddles. This ancient ritual of asking riddles had been a part of ancient cultures for centuries, and it is still evidenced in both history and mythology today. Asking riddles was considered to be an excellent test of the wisdom, intelligence, or education of another.

They exchanged pleasantries, and Makeda got straight to business. She called her attendants in, and they brought with them two vases of flowers, which they set down on the shining floor at the farthest end of the room. Her expression was openly and charmingly challenging the king to live up to his reputation as she told Solomon that one of the vases contained real flowers; the others had been skillfully made from fabric and other materials. His first riddle was to figure out which was which without rising from his throne.

Solomon didn't need to consider the question for long. He turned to his own attendants. "Open the window," he ordered.

Exchanging dubious glances, the attendants did as they were told. A warm breeze rushed through the room, running its fingers through Makeda's thick, dark hair. She watched in awe as a gentle buzzing filled the air, and one by one, bees came in from the hot sunshine, attracted by the smell of flowers. They went straight for the vase of real flowers and perched there, searching for the nectar, their delicate wings buzzing as they moved from one flower to the next.

Makeda tore her gaze away from the tiny insects to meet King Solomon's eyes. He didn't have to say anything. His smile said it all: he was ready for whatever she had to throw at him.

Through her wonder, Makeda pulled herself together. Over the buzzing of the bees, she asked her next question. "What is evil?" she asked.

Solomon's answer was instantaneous. "The eyes of the Lord in every place monitor good and evil, and in them is their definition."

Makeda paused. Tamrin had told her about this God that Solomon served. She wondered if He had anything to do with the confidence in the king's voice.

"What is the most powerful organ of the body?" she asked.

"Death and life are in the power of the tongue," said Solomon quickly with the certainty of a man whose single word could order an execution or begin a battle.

"Seven leave and nine enter," said Makeda. "Two pour out the draught, and only one drinks."

Solomon's eyes were intense, and Makeda realized that her heart was beating faster. "Seven are the days of a woman's menstruation," he said. "Nine are the months of her pregnancy. Her two breasts nourish the child, and the babe is the one that drinks."

Makeda grinned. Solomon was doing well, but she still had plenty of riddles up her sleeve for him. Yet in her heart, she knew that he'd already proven himself wise enough to teach her everything she wanted to know.

* * * *

Their visits continued on an almost daily basis. He would come to her, or she would go to him. She was always surrounded by attendants, yet every time Makeda looked at him, her heart would beat faster. She knew by the way that Solomon gazed at her that he felt the same, but she forced herself to stay focused on the task at hand. Makeda had come to learn wisdom so that she could govern Sheba wisely, not so that she could fall in love. Forcing the idea aside, she stayed attentive to what she was learning from him, and it awed her.

The precepts that the king taught her all centered on his God, and the more Makeda—a worshiper of the sun and moon, like the rest of her nation—heard from Solomon, the more she wanted to learn. He taught her lessons about humility and gentleness, showing her what it meant to govern a nation the likes of Israel the way he'd learned to do from his great father David, and also—according to the Ethiopian account—likening himself to a lowly laborer. He told Makeda that he was a man just like any other, but the more time she spent with him, the more she began to realize that he was unlike any other man she'd ever met. And judging by the stream of compliments he gave her, Solomon was just as taken with her.

Like David, Solomon had one great weakness, and also like his father, it was women. And Makeda, it would turn out, would be no different.

* * * *

Makeda had been living in the royal palace of Jerusalem for several months, and she knew that the time was coming when she would have to return to Sheba. Solomon, too, knew that the queen had to return to her country. By this point, she had learned much about ruling; she had also adopted the God of Israel as her own. According to Solomon, however, her instruction was not yet complete. He invited her into his own dining hall, ostensibly to show her the inner workings of his administration—but he also had an ulterior motive.

When Makeda came to the inner chambers, she was delighted to find that Solomon had set up a private space for her where she could see without being seen. It was as luxurious as everything else the king had done for her; there was purple draping, incense, and the heavenly scent of myrrh. She took her place there and spent all day watching as the king and his servants dined and met with other dignitaries.

It was late in the evening by the time everyone else left. Solomon approached Makeda's secret place and spoke with her. "Rest here until daybreak," he entreated her.

Makeda saw the gleam in his eyes. "Swear to me that you won't take me by force," she said. "I am a maiden—and I don't want to travel back to my people with the shame of losing my virginity in this way. Swear by your God, the God of Israel."

"I swear that I won't take you by force," Solomon agreed, "but you must swear that you won't take anything in my house."

Makeda shook her head, laughing. Why would she want to steal anything from Solomon, she asked, laughingly agreeing to his request. If she had known the plan behind what he asked, she would not have laughed.

Servants came in and readied the chamber for the two of them with Solomon's bed on one end and Makeda's on the other. But things would not stay this way for long. Craftily, Solomon had made sure that the last meal he'd served Makeda was salty and spicy, and when the queen woke in the night, she found herself with a burning thirst. She spotted a bowl of water in the chamber and sighed with relief. Getting up, she padded over to the bowl and lifted it to her lips.

That was when Solomon rose, startling the queen. His eyes flickered with delight. "Why have you broken your oath?" he demanded.

We will never know what exactly was going through Makeda's mind at that moment. Was she afraid? Did she realize what she had done with horror or with a secret joy?

Either way, the result was the same. "I've sinned against you," she told Solomon. "You are free from your oath."

And Solomon took her hand and led her to bed.

Chapter 8 – Joy on the Journey Home

Illustration II: A 17th-century artist's impression of the Queen of Sheba leaving Israel. While the Kebra Nagast has the queen travel by camel, some accounts say that she arrived in Israel by ship.

Sheba beckoned, but Makeda found herself hesitating as she stood in a hidden nook just outside the royal palace of Jerusalem. This time, her entourage for the journey home was vast. Six thousand camels stood waiting, ready to start the long trip back to Sheba, and they were so laden with everything that Makeda could have desired—precious metals, gemstones, beautifully embroidered garments—that six thousand was almost not enough. Makeda was about to bring a tremendous gift home to her people, and it was not only in the form of the material things that the camels bore. Her mind and heart were filled with the instructions that Solomon had given her, and she was excited to get back home and apply everything that she had learned.

Yet she still found herself hovering, a little reluctant to get on her camel and leave. Secreted away just outside the palace, she gazed up into Solomon's enchanting eyes, and memories of the night they'd spent together stirred in her heart.

Solomon had taken her aside for a moment, out of the loud musical ceremony with which he was seeing her off. His dark eyes gleamed as he worked the delicate ring off his little finger and held it out to her. "Take this so that you'll never forget me," he murmured, sliding it over her finger. "And if it so be that you bear a son to me, let this ring be a sign to him, and let him come to me." He paused, emotion clouding his face, knowing that he might never see the beautiful queen again. "Remember everything that I've told you, and worship God with all your heart, and perform His will."

Makeda knew that this was goodbye. She was ready to go home, but she knew that a great piece of her heart would stay behind with this bewitching king.

"May God be with you," said Solomon roughly. "Go in peace."

So, Makeda walked away from him, the only man she'd ever loved. She got on her camel and turned back to Sheba, and as the camel walked away, she felt the stirrings of a new life deep inside her.

* * * *

The long journey back to Sheba grew more and more arduous for the pregnant queen. With the thousands of camels to manage, there always seemed to be something slowing them down, and Makeda grew more and more anxious as her belly swelled with every passing day. She was not going to be able to give birth to her child in Sheba. Instead, to her horror, she realized that she was going to bring her firstborn forth somewhere along the way.

The pains of labor seized her nine months and five days after she'd left the safety of Jerusalem. Attended by a nurse—not the medical professional that the nurses of today are, but a woman who was ready to nurse Makeda's child on her behalf—the young queen was forced to birth her baby somewhere along the road, although she would possibly have been able to stop in a city. Still, she would have been surrounded by strangers with no family and possibly no friends nearby; apart from the baby that was making its entrance into the world, Makeda had no family. She would only have this child, and she had to birth it alone, with no medications and no help.

Makeda knew that she would likely never journey back to Jerusalem again. She also knew that there would never be another man for her, not after Solomon. The future of her entire kingdom hinged upon the birth of this child, and when, finally, the nurse placed the baby into Makeda's arms, she could only rejoice as she laid eyes on the healthy little baby. What was more, it was a little boy. Sheba now had a male heir.

The baby's name depends on the account you read; in Muslim accounts, he was known as Ibn al-Hakim, or the "Son of the Wise," while in the *Kebra Nagast*, he was Bayna-Lehkem. In history, however, he is most popularly known by his simplest name: Menelik, later Menelik I.

With the baby being safely cared for by the nurse, Makeda journeyed home to a country that welcomed her and her infant son with open arms. Menelik was illegitimate under Jewish law, but the people of Sheba had little regard for such things; a son was a son, and they welcomed him home as their crown prince. They were delighted to see their queen again and were especially excited to see the gifts she brought home. Wealthy and prosperous Sheba was not only even wealthier and more prosperous now—its queen was home, and the whole country rejoiced.

* * * *

Twelve-year-old Menelik had grown up surrounded by nothing but the best. His mother made sure that he had everything his heart desired—and several things that his heart certainly didn't. Chief among these was an education. Menelik would far rather have been out riding and hunting than stuck in the opulent rooms of the palace, listening to his tutors drone on and on about subjects that bored him. But he dutifully attended his lessons because his mother told him that he would be king one day.

The only good thing about lessons, from Menelik's point of view, was his friends. He had grown up among a group of noble boys his age, and they played, fought, and fooled around together. One thing he always noticed was how the other boys all had fathers. Some of their fathers had died in battles or accidents, but even those boys spoke of them often, and Menelik couldn't understand why he didn't have a father. He eventually began to ask, and his shy curiosity led him to ask his friends before anyone else.

"Who is my father?" he asked them one day as they were walking through the palace, the other boys pushing and jostling as they teased each other.

"Solomon the King," one of the boys answered him.

Menelik's father was a king? He had to find out more. He hurried back to his mother and asked her about it at the first opportunity.

Makeda was dismayed when Menelik asked her who his father was. She turned the ring that Solomon had given her around and around on her finger, knowing that Menelik's curiosity about his father might lead him all the way to Israel, and she knew from experience how long that journey was.

She stared at the boy. It had been almost thirteen long years since she'd turned away from the palace at Jerusalem and the man who'd captured her heart, and with every day that passed, Menelik looked more and more like his father. He had those same eyes, intense and serious, and even all these years later, Makeda felt an agonizing pang of longing for the king she'd loved. She couldn't let Menelik go. He was all that she had left of Solomon and of her own family. "I am your father and your mother," she said angrily, trying to scare him into dropping the subject.

But Menelik didn't let it go. He continued to pester and pester his mother until she finally told him. "His country is far away, and the road there is very difficult; wouldn't you rather stay here?" she asked.

Possibly seeing how his questioning had grieved his mother, Menelik let it go.

But not for long.

Chapter 9 – A New King

Makeda knew the moment that Menelik walked in that she couldn't put it off any longer. Her boy was going to Israel, and there was little that she could do to stop him.

She gazed at him with sorrow, remembering the day—ten years ago now—that he'd first asked her about his father. She'd been just as terrified to lose him then as she was now, but now he wasn't a boy anymore but a strong young man. He had his father's broad shoulders and pure voice; the flash of his eyes held the same intelligence, and Makeda knew that he'd grown into a worthy young prince. Yet the prince's heart longed to know more about where he had come from. He had grown up hearing the stories about his mother's family, but his father was a stranger to him except for the awed whispers of everyone who knew the story of Solomon's wisdom and how he had imparted it to Queen Makeda. His questioning heart wouldn't rest until he'd seen his father's face.

Menelik saw his mother's sorrow in her eyes. He spoke to her gently. "I will go and look upon the face of my father," he told her, "and I will come back here by the will of God, the Lord of Israel."

Makeda smiled. He sounded so much like Solomon when he talked about God; she had raised him according to Solomon's teachings, after all. She called for Tamrin, and he limped into the room. Even more grizzled now than he had been a quarter of a century earlier when he made his first trip to Israel, Tamrin was still faithfully serving the queen as the chief of her merchants. "Get ready for your journey," she told him. "And take this young man with you, because he won't stop asking me to go. Take him to the King and bring him back here in safety, if God wills it."

* * * *

King Solomon stood in his royal palace gazing out of the window at the great city of Jerusalem. The mighty Holy Temple, completed years ago, towered above the other buildings in its splendor and grandeur; within, Solomon had seen the presence of God and had hidden a thousand holy treasures, including the Ark of the Covenant. The holiest of all holy objects, the Ark contained numerous holy items, including the tablets on which the Ten Commandments had been written. It was hidden deep within the temple in an inner chamber where only the high priest ever entered, which was only on the rarest of occasions.

The Ark was not the only treasure that Solomon had gathered in Jerusalem. His stables were filled with the best and proudest Egyptian horses; his houses overflowed with women, as he was now married to 700 wives and had 300 concubines. Although he had had little luck with children, at least he did have a seven-year-old heir, little Rehoboam. His treasuries were filled with the most elaborate riches, and his coffers were spilling over with gold. Even his mind and heart were filled with the most precious and priceless thing of all: wisdom. Yet there was one thing that the richest king on Earth wanted, one beautiful treasure that he had been missing for decades, and her name was Makeda. He wondered where she was now, if she had even made it safely home to Sheba. If she remembered him the way that he remembered her.

There was a commotion outside, and King Solomon turned around to find a few wide-eyed palace guards hurrying into the room. Spies had come to the palace from the province of Gaza, they said, and they had a very perplexing reason for riding to Jerusalem: they were coming to see if King Solomon was in his palace because, according to some of the people of Gaza, the king was in Gaza.

Infuriated, Solomon ordered the spies to be brought to him and explain themselves. There must be an impostor in Gaza, and who knows what trouble such an individual was going to cause.

The spies were brought before Solomon, and he demanded to know their story. Trembling, one of the spies threw himself on the ground in front of the king. "Hail, may the royal father live!" he exclaimed nervously. "Our country is disturbed, because a merchant has come to it that looks exactly like you in every way, without the smallest alteration or variation."

Solomon listened to the spy describing this merchant, and hope leaped in his heart. The similarity that the spy talked about was such that Solomon knew that there was only one reasonable explanation: The man had to be his son. His son by the Queen of Sheba, the woman that Solomon's heart had always longed for.

* * * *

Solomon sent the commander of his army, Benaiah, to Gaza with all haste, ordering him to bring the young man to the palace as quickly as possible. Menelik found himself being ushered to Jerusalem as fast as Benaiah could bring him; Solomon was desperate to see him, and when he finally laid eyes on his firstborn, he was awed and delighted. The entire court was struck speechless by the resemblance between father and son.

Immediately, Solomon decided to make it his business to hold on to Menelik for all he was worth. He had let the Queen of Sheba herself slip through his fingers, but he wasn't about to let the same thing happen with his oldest child. Bestowing countless gifts on Menelik, including gorgeous garments embroidered with gold, Solomon practically begged him to stay. He wanted to make Menelik the King of Israel, and for a young man whose future lay wide open before him, it must have been a tempting proposition.

But back home in Sheba, there was an aging queen pining for her boy, the only family she had left. And Menelik remembered his promise to his mother. Despite Solomon's continued entreaties, Menelik held firm: he was going home to Sheba, just as he'd promised. He had not come to Israel in order to be made its king. He had come to meet his father, and he had one request to ask of him: that he would be crowned as the King of Sheba using Israelite rituals and ceremonies. The request was not entirely Menelik's; instead, Queen Makeda herself had asked for this to be done so that Sheba would be ruled by a king who had been consecrated and made holy, just like the King of Israel whom she loved so fiercely.

King Menelik I left Jerusalem to an outpouring of dismay. Solomon had done as Makeda had asked and crowned Menelik the King of Sheba with tremendous pomp and ceremony; the high priest in the temple himself had given Menelik instructions for his rule. What was more, Solomon sent Menelik home with the firstborns of all his nobles in order for them to rule in Sheba just as their families ruled in Israel. It was a great procession that left for Sheba, and while Menelik and his friends rejoiced, all of Jerusalem wept and howled at the loss of the young man who could have been King of Israel. According to some accounts, it was not just himself and the other young people that Menelik took back to Sheba. The Ark of the Covenant itself was included in the list of treasures that Menelik had in his procession, smuggled out of the temple by some of Menelik's retinue. The *Kebra Nagast* tells how an angel told them to steal the Ark and carry it off to Sheba, and to this day, Ethiopia claims to have the Ark hidden in a tiny chapel in the village of Aksum, guarded by devoted monks who are never allowed to set foot outside the chapel until the day they die.

So, Menelik returned to Sheba and to a great rejoicing. Sheba had gained not only a newly anointed king but also a vast array of young nobles who had grown up at the feet of Solomon's wisdom. Makeda was overjoyed to have her son back. She surrendered her throne to him, and a son of Solomon sat down upon the throne of Sheba, of Ethiopia. There was great rejoicing, and the whole palace was filled with a joyous celebration.

As for Makeda herself, the beautiful, wise, and courageous Queen of Sheba, her story faded into obscurity once her son took the throne. She had gone to Jerusalem for wisdom to protect her country, and now, she had proven that she had done even better than that: She had brought home an heir educated like one of Israel's greatest kings, an heir whose coronation promised peace and safety for Sheba in the generations to come. Makeda had fulfilled her mission to protect her people.

Wisdom was not all that she had found in Israel, though. She watched the celebration and gazed at her son upon the throne. He was in every way the image of his father, and when she closed her eyes, she could still see the gleam in Solomon's dark eyes that night. A night that she would never forget.

Conclusion

Almost nothing is known of Makeda's life after the coronation of Menelik. We can only guess that her devoted son ensured that she lived out her days in peace and safety in the country that she'd done everything to protect; yet perhaps a part of her longed forever for the man she'd left behind in Jerusalem decades ago.

The story of the Queen of Sheba is an incomplete one. We only have an educated guess at where Sheba was even located; historians doubt whether the queen herself ever existed. Accounts differ wildly on all but one thing—she came to King Solomon for wisdom, even though her own country was filled with riches, and she was tremendously impressed.

Ethiopian tradition, however, is utterly assured of the fact that her son with King Solomon was not only a king of Ethiopia—he was also the progenitor of a dynasty that, according to tradition, lasted nearly 3,000 years. Sheba became Aksum whose rulers' obscure origins makes it possible that they were, in fact, descendants of Menelik. In the Middle Ages, the Zagwe dynasty briefly took over ruling Aksum after murdering the entire royal family, apart from a single baby that was smuggled out of danger by supporters. The Zagwe dynasty was overthrown in 1270 by Yekuno Amlak, who claimed to be a descendant of Menelik, and with his rule, the official Solomonic Dynasty began.

Solomonic emperors would rule over Aksum, which became known as Ethiopia, for centuries. In fact, it was only during the Second World War that Ethiopia was invaded and occupied for the first time since the time of the Zagwes; Mussolini's Italian troops occupied the country only briefly, and the emperor, Haile Selassie, was sent into exile. Selassie was the last of the Solomonic emperors. He was deposed in 1974 and died in prison a year later.

Solomon's descendants no longer sit on the Ethiopian throne; democracy was instituted after Selassie's deposition, allowing presidents to be elected and to govern the country in a fairer and more modern manner. Yet there still remains something intensely poetic about the current president, something that connects the ancient rule of the Queen of Sheba with the Ethiopia of today. Like the fabled queen, Sahle-Work Zewde is a striking African woman proudly ruling over a magnificent country. She is the only female head of state on the entire continent.

The Queen of Sheba remains a historical figure so wreathed in mystery that she is little more than a legend. Yet her tale of courageous rule, in a time when women were denied power, and of her selfless protection of her people has a powerful quality that still makes her an inspiration thousands of years later. We might never know the real story behind the Queen of Sheba. But the story we do have—a story of a brave queen who would do anything for her people—promises to continue to ring down through the generations to come.

Here's another book by Captivating History that you might be interested in

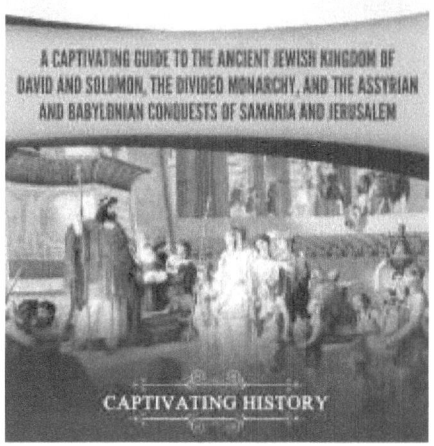

And another one...

Sources

The Holy Bible, King James Version (https://www.biblegateway.com/)

Kebra Nagast, as translated by Sir E. A. Wallis Budge (http://www.yorku.ca/inpar/kebra_budge.pdf)

http://jhodgesagame.blogspot.com/2013/07/the-queen-of-sheba-kingdom-of-dmt-and.html

https://www.britannica.com/place/Ethiopia/Sports-and-recreation#ref419469

https://theancientweb.com/explore/africa/ethopia/

https://www.ancient.eu/Kingdom_of_Saba/

https://www.africa.com/great-ancient-african-queens/

http://freemasonry.bcy.ca/texts/gmd1999/sheba.html

https://www.pbs.org/mythsandheroes/myths_four_sheba.html

http://www.womeninthebible.net/women-bible-old-new-testaments/queen-of-sheba/

http://www.blackhistoryinthebible.com/blurred-lines/king-menelik-i-the-solomonic-dynasty-and-the-ark-of-the-covenant/

https://www.geni.com/people/Menelik-I-da-Ethiopia/6000000002518586281

https://www.japantimes.co.jp/life/2013/06/30/travel/how-the-ark-of-the-covenant-got-to-ethiopia/#.XOzftLPv7ak

https://www.theguardian.com/lifeandstyle/2010/oct/09/haile-selassie-ethiopia-king-solomon

https://www.britannica.com/topic/Solomonid-dynasty

https://ethiopianhistory.com/Solomonic_Dynasty/

https://www.nytimes.com/1986/02/04/science/was-there-a-queen-of-sheba-evidence-makes-her-more-likely.html

https://www.aljazeera.com/news/2018/10/sahle-work-zewde-ethiopia-female-president-181027134726828.html

Illustration I: The Queen of Sheba from a manuscript (Staats- und Universitätsbibliothek Göttingen, 2 Cod. Ms. Philos. 63, Cim., fol. 122r) of Bellifortis by Conrad Kyeser.
https://commons.wikimedia.org/wiki/File:Bellifortis_Queen_of_Sheba.jpg

Illustration II: By Giovanni Demin (1789-1859) - http://www.artrenewal.org/pages/artwork.php?artworkid=10389, Public Domain, https://commons.wikimedia.org/w/index.php?curid=3520809

Illustration III: By Claude Lorrain (1605-1682)
https://en.wikipedia.org/wiki/File:Claude_Lorrain_008.jpg

www.ingramcontent.com/pod-product-compliance
Lightning Source LLC
LaVergne TN
LVHW090039080526
838202LV00046B/3884